portraits of red and gray

portraits of red and gray

memoir poems

james c. morehead

Apart from the well-known actual people, events, and locales that figure in the narrative, all names, characters, places, and incidents in this book are the products of the author's imagination or are used fictitiously. Any resemblance to current events or locales, or to living persons, is entirely coincidental.

Published in the United States by Viewless Wings Press, Dublin, California.

Library of Congress Control Number: 2021924008

Paperback ISBN 978-1-7367890-2-5

viewlesswingspress.com

10 9 8 7 6 5 4 3 2 1

First Edition

Cover and book design: Zoe Norvell | Cover art: Igor Prilutsky (lithograph, 1982)

Editing: Mary Morehead and Philip Morehead | Copy Editing: Brittany Smail

Table of Contents

INTRODUCTION

Poetry is crafted using many sources of inspiration. Some poems start with an image, sound, scent, or emotion. Some poems are pure invention. This book is built on my memories, a collection of memoir poems that, despite being personal, capture universal experiences.

In choosing poems for my first book, *canvas: poems,* I included a few excerpts from my long poem *portraits of red and gray* (about a high school trip in 1983 to the USSR). Multiple readers asked to see the entire poem, which motivated creating this book.

This collection of memoir poems brings universal themes to life through journeys to the USSR and the mountains of Tuscany, the concert halls in San Francisco and a tiny town in Wyoming, the cables of Yosemite's Half Dome and the beaches of Normandy.

The New Yorkers

Visiting last fall I noticed the *New Yorker* on your kitchen counter
our issues identical but for the address boxes:
one marked *California*, well lit by endless sun;
the other *Lake of Bays*, burrowed deep in pine.

I wonder, do we skip the same reviews,
ponder the same poems, laugh at the same cartoons?
Do you display a curated selection of covers
on your coffee table and bathroom magazine rack?

When I was younger I would sit cross-legged
among your colorful unread stacks.
So many words left to learn, I thought,
as I thumbed through another issue.

As I walk back from the mailbox,
my copy buried in a pile of bills,
I imagine you lingering in bed,
hiding from mom, finishing one last page.

I begin with "FICTION" and wonder,
are you searching for "FICTION" too?
Or have you fallen back asleep,
as the pages slip through your fingers?

That Summer in Savery, Wyoming

Speeding along WY-70
alone in the back of my aunt's Audi.

The Savery, Wyoming, sign claims **population 25**—
I guess I could meet them all if I tried.

I've brought my Boston busyness,
expecting every minute to be filled.

Instead my cousin spends hours making flies.
I learn they are for fooling fish.

I read through every book he owns,
some twice.

I flip the Billy Joel cassette over,
and over.

I'm awoken by a rooster to
collect eggs each morning,
reaching under the soft of hens.

I explore every corner of the dusty, manure-scented barns.

I watch a family of foxes pop up, then scurry
when I'm hiking near their den.

I build a spaceship from discarded wood.

I mow the front lawn for an afternoon,
amusing my aunt.
It was a field, not a lawn.

I spend hours spelling horse with a basketball.

I silently watch as my uncle bales hay,
his crisp Stetson a silhouetted shadow in noon sun.

I ask about the cattle guards as we rattle in his F-150.

I walk to the General Store, searching for candy.

I do other things,
and nothing,
for hours and days and weeks.

When night falls,
I fall asleep,
lulled by the quiet of Wyoming.

NORMANDY (in 9 scenes)

1. BUSINESS TRIP DETOUR

I head out alone, when meetings end, on the TGV speeding west. From *la tour Eiffel* to Normandy's coast, scenes flutter by in a blur.

2. DISEMBARK FOR CHOCOLAT

My rollerboard rattles to a quaint hotel in Caen. *Moelleux au chocolat* awaits, and with a nudge, the center flows, molten on my plate.

3. UP AT DAWN

The directions are unfolded, in near-English and French: "Arrive precisely at 9:00 - *Le Mémorial de Caen*." Steady rain. Shivers. The streets are mostly empty. The *Citroën* departs.

4. NONE BUT ONE

The meeting place is empty; perhaps I botched the time. But sure enough and on the dot the tour guide arrives. I'm forty-something, six foot five, the guide petite and—half my age? An awkward pause as she looks up; a French knot scarf is tied *just so*. Her voice is firm, Parisian tones, *Do you mind the rain?* (I think she hopes I'll quit the tour, but I am not deterred.) Resigned, she turns, clipboard in hand, and leads me to her van.

5. THEY HEAD WEST

I sit up front by textbook stacks, empty rows behind. Driving west past Bayeux, picturesque and calm, the guide speaks softly and begins, *that town was spared during the war, this other one fully destroyed.*

6. THE WHITE CROSSES

I wander through the countless rows, white crosses set in green. Below *cimetière américain,* the Channel within reach, *Saving Private Ryan* scenes.

But the beaches now are hedgehog-free: two lovers walking hand in hand, a fisherman by lines of rods, anchored in gray sand. Later my guide whispers, *this is my favorite place, "mélancolie," a quiet space.*

7. WHERE RANGERS SCALED

Where we go next is up to you, so I ask her to suggest. *In that case, off to Pointe du Hoc,* not sure what to expect. She tells me tales of Army Rangers, scaling cliffs, then trapped for days; German soldiers tucked in bunkers. We climb down into burrowed craters blasted long ago. *Since the war*, she observes, *nothing here will ever grow.*

8. THE BLACK CROSSES

She starts to drive back towards Caen, the rain slowing to mist. *There's one more place I recommend, it's not part of the tour.* I signal *yes,* we park near some hedges, unkempt and nondescript. *This graveyard's for forgotten soldiers, not marked on any map; each plot holds Germans two or three, buried in a stack.* I pause among the unnamed crosses, each simply carved in black.

9. WHITE AND BLACK

Now it's time, she checks her watch as we turn to leave. Through the windshield fields pass by, each filled with crosses black and white, their arms outstretched and drenched in mist, each waiting for the clouds to lift.

echoes in the nave

there are three of us
not yet ten with voices unbroken
new recruits fidgeting nervously
the choirmaster
                    sitting
                    postured
                    upright
one hand at the piano
the other directing drills
to train our soprano vocals

            ooo ahhh ooo
            eee ohhh eee
    in-egg-shell-see-us-day-oh

we hold each note until we gasp
our ears perked for wavering tones
when we slip out of tune

in time we graduate from pitch and chords
to balancing black folders in perfect Vs
containing this week's hymns and psalms
(and, if we're lucky, benjamin britten)

    sunday morning

we arrive early at st. paul's
before the parishioners come
gathering in the robing room

checked in by a stern glance
swapping overcoats for black pleated cloth
then taking our places behind the chancel door

into the vaulted hall we march
singing as we step two by two
arms raised! eyes up!
inspected as we pass the altar
the peal and drone from towering pipes
ringing in our ears

we reach the wooden stalls
carved ornate some years ago
and in a mirror across the aisle
i follow the baton's direction
until with a flourished wave
we sit

while the priest reads
from a well-thumbed ribbon-marked book
i scan the pews
filled with rows of lowered heads
and wonder
did they hear my voice as i entered
or was i lost in the echoes of the nave?

Four Summers in Florida (82-83-84-85)

1982

I spent my teenage summers working in Florida, living alone, programming computers. That was forty years ago, when parents let their sons fly two thousand miles south, from Toronto to Florida, to live alone, and program computers all summer.

I was fifteen and couldn't drive, so I brought a hand-me-down bike with saddlebags for carrying groceries. That was forty years ago, when parents let their sons live alone, without a car, two thousand miles away. At least my parents did, I can't speak for other parents.

The company hired me because of a family connection but kept me because I was a good computer programmer. (I'd be called a coder now.) They put me up in a motel in Largo, Florida. I had one week to find a place to live. (If you haven't heard of Largo, don't worry, I hadn't either; it's near Tampa.) That first night, standing at a payphone in the motel parking lot, under a buzzing streetlight, homesickness enveloping me, I had to wait for my tears to dry before dropping in quarters to call home.

I worked 9 to 5. At night, alone in the motel, with cicadas singing in sticky air, I circled *rooms for rent* in the classifieds, newsprint staining my fingertips (this was before the internet, and browsers, and phones that weren't pay phones, and Craigslist). I learned things: you need to lie about your age when you are fifteen and trying to rent a room. But I was tall, and people trusted me. Or I was good at bullshitting. Or both.

I ended up renting a room in a house owned by an elderly woman with emphysema. She told me it was because she smoked too much. She lived alone, and enjoyed having me to talk to. I was alone, and enjoyed talking to her too. I mostly ate Kraft dinner, while watching TV.

I rode the hand-me-down bike everywhere. I rode to work in the Florida sun that turned water into steam, and soaked everything I wore. I changed into dry clothes in a cramped bathroom stall at work. I rode in the rain, tucked under the awning of the Circle K, waiting for thunderstorms to pass. I rode at night, my bike's headlamp flickering a path home.

Everyone at work was an adult and they called me the *Pac-Man Kid*. I was called the *Pac-Man Kid* because every day, after work, I'd stop at an arcade and spend hours playing video games. I mostly played a tennis game because I was so good. I could play for an hour with one quarter. I guess they should have called me the *Tennis Kid*.

For my sixteenth birthday my coworkers got me a Pac-Man cake, and someone took a photo. (It's the only photo I have from those four summers in Florida. In the photo I'm dressed for work: a collared shirt, sleeves rolled up, checkbook in my breast pocket. It must have been the day I went to the bank, because of the checkbook. I would ride my bike up to the drive-thru window to deposit my paycheck. The teller would recognize me and smile. Or perhaps she was smiling because I was on my bike in the drive-thru lane.)

1983

As the second summer approached, my friends talked about going to the Police Picnic (a festival featuring the band the Police, not police officers). My friends would invite me to come, forgetting I'd be in Florida all summer. I always left before my birthday, with the ink barely dry on my report card.

My bike was left behind in Toronto; a Delta 88 took its place, borrowed for the summer. I could say it was a vintage car, but that would be bullshitting. The *clunker* burned a can of oil for every tank of gas, and on a good day lumbered without stalling.

I lived in a motel, in a single room, with a small fridge and a few elements for boiling things. And a TV for filling the quiet hours. The motel was plain, but across the street there was a public pool where I would escape the humidity and swim laps while local teenagers chatted and laughed. I wanted to chat and laugh too. I kept swimming, though, until it was time to walk back to my room.

I went to work and wrote more computer programs. A couple of the engineers once took me to Hooters for lunch. I was probably blushing when ordering.

I drove to Orlando one weekend and spent the day in EPCOT. I was getting lots of practice being alone. I wore headphones, listening to the Human League's "Dare" on my Walkman, flipping the tape over and over while people watching behind sunglasses. My shorts only had room for one tape.

1984

The company put me up for a week in the house of the CEO's son. The son was a former drug addict who had found God and led evangelical Christian prayer circles. I eavesdropped from upstairs and decided I didn't need to be saved, but I lowered my head tactfully before meals.

I lived in a beauty salon that summer. Rather, I lived in a rented room *behind* the beauty salon. There was a pool outside my room, and the owner's daughter, back from college, sunbathed in a bikini; her perfectly smooth skin turned a bit darker each day. I may have said "hi." I don't remember swimming that summer, unsure of parading my scrawny frame by her college-toned body. The Olympics came and went, with Mary Lou Retton's perfect 10 vault to take the gold. I watched Mary Lou when I wasn't sneaking glances at the bikini girl.

I had a real work friend now. His name was Dave. (I've had several friends named Dave, or at least some are Daves, others are Davids. This one was Dave.) He drove a vintage VW Bug. It was *vintage* in the same way the Delta 88 I drove in 1983 was *vintage*. His car had a rusted out hole in the floor that was covered by a piece of plywood to keep out downpours. Dave taught me about solenoids. The cassette tape player in my loaner car didn't work: tapes wouldn't stay in—turned out it was the solenoid.

The Go-Go's and INXS played a concert that summer. I stood in the pit watching the girls rush the stage for INXS and the boys rush for the Go-Go's (back then security was light and you could rush the stage). Driving home the encore echoed in my ears.

1985

The last summer approached. I'd just graduated from high school, had a fake ID, and watched my new girlfriend head north to be a camp counselor. I hoped she'd still be my girlfriend when I returned. I borrowed the family station wagon and drove south with my mom. I dropped her off in Tennessee for a conference filled with oboists (my mom is an oboist). When we stopped for food, the accents were so thick we had to order with question marks.

I rented a room in a mansion with a Rolls-Royce, waxed and gleaming, parked out front. The owner lived alone, had two grown sons, and before he came out years ago, a wife. In the room across from me, a recent divorcee was in between lives. She didn't stay long.

That was the summer of Live Aid. I took over the living room TV, watching Phil Collins take the Concorde from London to Philadelphia, and Queen perform "Radio Ga Ga." I recorded the concert on my boombox, swapping tapes between sets, then mixing and remixing them. (I lost those tapes long ago.)

In my room I had a turntable. Instead of quarters in arcades, I spent dollars in record stores. I saved up for vinyl, carefully unwrapping each album, examining the cover, tilting until the sleeve peeked out, hoping for liner notes, then placing side A and lowering the needle.

I used my fake ID one Saturday night. I drove across the Howard Frankland Bridge to Tampa, to a dance club. I sat at the bar. A pretty woman sat down next to me and said "hi." I bullshitted and said I was a college student with a summer job. I offered to buy her a drink, and she said "no," so I drank it and another one—and one more, and we kept talking until I realized I was in over my head. I said I had to pee and I hid in the bathroom for a long time, then snuck out and slept in my car. I was too terrified to drive. The windows fogged up from the humidity. There was tapping on the glass and people pointing and laughing. When morning came I drove in the right lane, under the speed limit, checking the mirror for flashing lights. I wonder what would have happened if I'd kept talking to the woman at the bar.

And then the summer ended. I drove north.

as we paused on the cables

we leave in darkness
guided by headlamp beams
and the
          tsh
               tsh
          tsh
of boots on gravel

we hike for hours through waterfall mist
up stone-carved steps in forest depths
lit by hints of sunrise glow
past cottonwood and oak
until in time our muscles ache

then breaking through the tree line's edge
lit brilliant as the shadows flee
switchbacks in stone go farther up
and in the distance, anchored firm
a pair of cables—two sleek lines
appear on half dome's spine

we join the queue, anxious, unsure
then cling to steel and start to climb
on cooled magma, slick as frost
from winters' rain in years before

and then my calf begins to cramp

i pause for breath

suspended on a weathered plank
your camelbak just steps ahead

you turn and ask
are you okay?

and so i say,

we're almost there
we'll be okay
i can see the summit now

and then

and then

i'm holding you, only just born
cradled up, so perfect, slight
my teary eyes begin to blur
time disconnects—i won't let go
your sleeping breath so softly slows

for emily

into the heart of temagami

#1

mom leaves us by the dock
with sleeping-bag bundles
rain slicks boots scarves
doubled socks flashlights
aspirin tums cough syrup
a few hugs a wave goodbye
then dad and i wait for our motorboat taxi
anxious to enter
temagami

---

base camp holds reminders of home
real toilets
two-ply paper
sinks running water real beds
mattresses
the wilderness on all sides doesn't seem real
we read and snooze and kick ass in ping-pong
as the other sons and fathers arrive
i wonder
why leave this behind
to sleep on a rock?

---

john and marty are in charge
we help them load ten days of food
into tightly packed wooden boxes
they call them *wannigans*

salted meat
portioned cereal
pancake mix dry milk
carefully sorted ordered layers
each layer a meal
each serving
assigned

---

john leads us to the dock
and a line of waiting wooden canoes

" step in
steady...
don't stand up!
use both hands
stay low "

we paddle in rhythmic strokes
pull in
sweep out
leaving vortexes swirling behind us

we practice capsizing
dad and i cling to the gunwale

wave

breathe

wait

until canoes surround us
pulling us out chilled

and dripping

our mighty rescuers tumble over
joining the waterlogged victims
cursing at the bare-bottomed canoes
and splashing bobbing heads

#2

night falls slowly
on an evening in deep summer
hours before our departure
i wander out alone
to watch the canoes
                                        slumbering silently
and run my fingers along
the smooth wooden skin

---

a predawn clanging bell
and fumbling through dew-soaked blackness
to lift the canoes from their beds
                                                            grumbling
then slide them over sand
into crisp water that chills me awake
through my feet legs spine

---

we begin
gliding across the lake
my fingers hands arms joined with the paddle
pulling forward repeating endlessly

i swallow the air
guzzling deep delicious gulps
i feel the near silence
no sirens tire skids engines horns tvs machines
just the caress of breeze

as we dip and pull
leaving blue ripples behind us

---

we're signaled to shore
a campsite hidden between towering pines
and a swarm of insects

the fathers (try to) cook
john and marty gather wood
building a fire until it pops

dinner tastes like ash and smoke
every drink of bug juice wiggles
i've never tasted food so wonderful
i've never felt so tired

we compete for clear land
our tents appear
one by one
tiny pyramids under an infinite blanket of night
the solid rock beneath me dad snoring beside
i can't hold myself awake
leaving darkness behind

#3

it's my turn to help gather firewood
marty slings an axe over his shoulder
and we cross to an island

i follow him silently
                                        ignorant
watching from a distance
as his blade rips into a dead pine
severed
                falls
                        crashing
i scurry with logs
filling the canoe
and avoiding marty's swinging axe
                                                                                        awed

---

we approach our first portage
i carefully choose the lightest box
then strap it to my forehead with a tumpline
the fathers balance canoes above them
heads hidden
i try not to laugh at these four-legged creatures

we walk for hours
                                    it seems
how far is a mile?
my mouth too dry to ask

#4

our next campsite is barren rock
barely alive
trees cling to small patches of soil
we lie back after supper on pure canadian shield
our stomachs full of potatoes cured meat marshmallows
the darkness pinpointed by a thousand stars
freed from the city's blazing light
i follow satellites
arcs from meteor trails
and connect the dots of ancient figures

---

dawn
our canoes enter the river's mouth
and we are swallowed by a tangle of branches
my father guides us through the twisted maze
we duck under fallen trees
the forest blurs sunlight into a rich green
i just read heart of darkness in school
i scan the shore for kurtz

#5

our last night
the sky is black with storm clouds
we eat dinner quickly
expecting rain
a tent flies from its anchors—
we chase it
laughing
then wrap ourselves in plastic sheets
as a wall of water approaches
lit in flashes by lightning

the storm passes and clouds crumble
uncovering sunshine
and sunset
we follow the storm's back
as a rainbow trails behind
its colors stretching
from treetops to water's edge

---

we push off one more time
into lazy swirls of mist that float across the lake
our canoes slide forward
through water smooth as polished glass
i try not to breathe
fearing it will shatter

Torta di Riso

Easter morning—through the ducts
and weathered cracks sweet wisps drift
from Nonna's basement kitchen where
she kneads pastry into a textured shell.
Her fingers work, coarse and firm
as still-steaming rice waits nearby.

Details are added: a bit of this and that
no measuring spoons or written recipe.
I peek over her shoulder, frantically scribbling
How much was that Nonna?
She laughs, *this much,* pouring on instinct
until into the oven to bake and brown.

That was before, when I would join
Mary each year as the good *genero*
at the table, waiting patiently for
torta di riso and leaving extra space—
Nonna knowing I will eat too much
if not monitored closely.

Now I can only watch as Nonna
tilts the pan for the camera
steam rising out of the screen
drifting west from Toronto to San Francisco—
a pixelated slice hovering ethereal.
I dream of one more slice *per favore.*

Ode to Docs

Stiff leather
                    Steel toed
Air cushioned
                         Yellow stitched

I took my Docs everywhere:
   to the Diamond Club on Sherbourne
   to Maple Leaf Gardens for Purple Rain
   to the Silver Crown every Saturday night

It was 1988, my hair crimped, jet black
sprayed stiff like Robert Smith
(a reference photo by my mirror)

I stood for hours in those Docs
waiting for Love and Rockets to take the stage
   or Thomas Dolby
   or Depeche Mode
   or others I've long forgotten

I was tall and slender
and safe in those Docs
that signaled—*alternative*

When winter came
they gripped the ice
and in the rain they kept me dry

As I grow older, they do too
showing the scuffs of passing time
and one more crease with each step

When I pass a window display
and see Docs, all shiny and new
I'll pause, look down—and keep walking

And when I step into the Fillmore
you join me—all grown up
and beaming with the joy
of a Christmas morning
our Docs side by side
as the band takes the stage

For Evelyn

An Afternoon with Geese at Northern Illinois University

A gaggle of geese, a rabble on a ledge
honk like middle school oboists
yelling *fuck off* to all those below

More geese patrol in squadrons of Vs
preparing to head south before the first snow
to conquer more lawns or an 18th tee

The rested are up-front leading the way
while the others recharge
barely needing to flap their wings

I keep a watchful eye
avoiding their green-yellow debris
scattered across the quad

then step inside a museum
picturesque, with ivied stone
guarded by a mannequin:

  tall and chic
  powdered hair bouffant
  choker of barbed wire

wearing a dress draped from shock blankets
all crinkled silver and orange
with imprinted silhouettes of refugees

"Marie Antoinette Visits the Border" by Judith Joseph

reads a placard on the wall
while images of orphans
huddle nearby

I pause, unsettled
before heading outside
cautiously—checking the sky

portraits of red and gray

(russia 1983 no gorby perestroika or hint of democracy)

#1

marshie greets us
a salesman today
carrying brochures of russia
red with cathedrals mosques museum statues
and snow-tipped mountain tops

(marshie - our english teacher
cool among the strung out
hormone-driven schoolboys
seventeen years old
and reckless)

he needs fifteen of us
an eighteen-day adventure

(excited whispers fly
disheveled ties and ripped-seam blazers
our eyes light up
we ignore mom and dad's expected gasps
two thousand canadian dollars :
airfare hotel food expenses
into communist coffers)

we have to go
young impatient imaginations explode
dreams of faraway places
of sean connery and michael caine
(capitalist kings in a lesser land)

in a few days
excited whispers and red brochures
whither
but i hang on

my mind wanders each night
through glossy tourist snapshots
my dreamy russia enchanted
my dreams innocent
ignorant

---

i study russia for homework
waiting anxiously
library book history
tour book advice
what to wear
where to buy
rubles kopeks
and rules
don’t drink the water
or take pictures of bridges
trucks
soldiers
tanks

i pack my suitcase full
with black market currency :
cigarettes
buttons
gum
jeans
running shoes
cassettes

---

yyz toronto

fifteen camera-clad schoolboys
oxfords and school blazers
replaced by topsiders and gucci sweaters
we are surrounded by parents
excited nervous hugs and kisses
be careful see you
                        soon

---

i can't remember most of their names
or faces

only my roommate phil
                        passed out in a vodka swirl

and raoul
        eating black-market caviar
        breakfast lunch and midnight snack
and frank
        armed with two-thousand-dollar photo gear
        (he never learned how to focus)
and marshie
          buying us drinks drinking and ignoring :
          the perfect chaperone

#2

helsinki finland

goodbye finnair
goodbye capitalism
goodbye five-star hotel

we are walking toward an aeroflot jet
steep metallic steps lead into oval darkness
i am too tall
my head ducks
                    hair brushing the entrance
a stewardess greets us in russian
then english
                  then vanishes
we take our assigned seats
cramped close
knees bunched up
nostrils filled with the scent of russian soap
so sickly strong it coats my lungs
i try not to breathe

our jet leaves the runway
dropping beneath us
our fears worries thoughts of home
are emptied onto the tarmac below
school homework exams
lie scattered beneath us
                                    forgotten

#3

our pilot attacks heaven without mercy
racing for altitude
an ear-popping ascent ripping through clouds
i grip my seat
used to north american comfort

relief
the plane levels
cruising softly
brushing cloud tops

waiting
waiting
waiting

for the last possible moment to land
dive-bombing the runway
like a kamikaze dropping
popping my ears confused vertical vertigo

gripping the ground
relieved
russian arms to inspect me
armed and stone-faced

a young soldier in a box
his eyes passing back
and forth
from my passport to me
saying nothing
signaling another young soldier

their eyes through me

i try to stare back
i try not to sweat

#4

moscow bumps past
our bus rides potholed streets
bucking wheezing shaking
past gray towers
and a horizon of silent cranes (surrounding)

it is monday
                    noon
there is no traffic but the sidewalks bustle
a green-gray fur-topped stream

i look for color
for red revlon nail polish
  or rich white milk (it does the body good)
  or flashy silver corvettes
                                        to offset matchbox ladas

all my eyes find
are blank vacant spaces
i cannot look i cannot look away
the dirty glass between me
                                        and them

#5

we try to find the five stars

moscow's hotel cosmos
ten inviting glass doors
(a little grimy)
eight locked
one jammed
one opens

a quick briefing on keys and floor passes :

we require a pass to enter the hotel
a pass to get our room key
we must not leave *with* our key
or *without* our pass

onward to a row of elevators
nine green doors slid shut
(only three in good repair)

the green door opens
our floor
my roommate (phil) and i step out
ambushed in russian by an oldish woman
who sits to one side behind a table
and a box of neatly spaced keys
your passes please
we guess we hear

she clasps our passes
exchanging them for keys

“go left”

we go

confused

#6

vodka party!

stolichnaya
bottles in every hand
                    (pepper vodka
                      lemon vodka)
drink after drink after...

it's my first-ever drink
i'm not sure what to do
                    how much to swallow
it feels burning hot
               then fuzzy
(tastes horrible)

i feel my way along walls toward the bathroom
spinning
slumping
     (a loud shout? somewhere? knocking?)
back into marshie's room
crumbling into a corner
maybe it's late

later

i find my room door key fumbling fall
phil's in the can
          (for hours)
i'm banging on the door
he won't come out

pissing in a pop bottle
careful aim in desperation

flopping onto
                    i hope
a bed

falling into a pitch-black spiral
passing out

out

#7

a suspensionless bus
will not let me forget
last night's vodka party

moscow passes blurred
famous churches statues buildings museums
                                        (i can't remember)
until the shades of gray reveal

        red square

i walk on stones rich in history
my breath sucked out in open space
                                    (walls towering
                                      enclosing
                                      silent)

a tv image explodes before me
                              peter
                              jennings
                              live
                              from
                              moscow

i cannot see i cannot hear
the parades of missiles
or cries of revolution
                      but i feel them
                      beneath my feet

#8

we are lined up
silent respectful
fearful

lenin's tomb before us
hundreds ahead in line
good citizens on their yearly pilgrimage

glazed guards stifle our approach
a tomb of simple shining marble (a bunker)
a single entrance
poised bayonets line our path
we keep our hands at our sides
walk slowly
breathe silently

someone ahead scratches an ear
sharpened blades level from all sides
shouting in russian

the line stops waits and
continues
(false alarm)
i check my hands

gripping my pants

steps inside a downward spiral

a bulletproof-glass-encased shoe

leg

waist

chest

head

peculiar

preserved

waxy

unreal

#9

gum department store
moscow's eaton centre
a long glass tunnel lined with shops
(and little to buy)

i see soviet efficiency displayed before me :

1. a woman stands in line waiting for shoes
2. she waits and waits and chooses a pair
3. only to receive a slip of paper with its price
4. she takes this paper and stands in line
5. and gives a cashier the paper and money
6. she gets a receipt and stands in line
7. finally trading the receipt for her shoes

i step outside into sunlight
sunglasses hiding me
i notice a teenager
lagging behind
suspicious
i watch him
turning around i pass him (a test)
he follows
whispering from behind "'sunglasses 30 rubles"
"'50" i say (a good capitalist)
he vanishes
i think
i turn a corner
face-to-face before me
he's standing
a handful of bills

into my left
sunglasses
into his right
without a word
disappears

my wallet full
i search moscow streets
empty shops and greasy food pass by
my eyes uncovered squinting
breathing smog in downtown air forgetting
for a second
four thousand miles from toronto

---

across a square and traffic
a toy store
lined and filled
i'm drawn toward large wooden dolls
in wooden dolls
rounded rolling smiling faces
i pull them out and open
lining them up along a shelf
until a russian clerk scolds
and chases my dolls back to their shells

i turn and sigh to a young girl's giggling
across an aisle and smiling
i blush and turn and look
she's gone
i search the store
through bobbing heads

daydreaming of a young girl's smile
and listening for the sound of laughter

#10

a small classroom
neatly spaced rows of eyes
we introduce ourselves
                                        one by one
they respond
mira ivan peter anslov
tied together like paper dolls
neckties scarves skirts and suits
perfect polite cautious smiles

an english class
we sit and listen and
to our surprise feel lost
in flawless fashioned grammar
a language strange precise
                                             and lifeless

we cross and meet
to swap and give
buttons stickers badges postcards
they eagerly embrace our western trinkets
and humbly
please and thank you

#11

somewhere in moscow a circus spiral-tarp-topped bubbles streams of parents grasp young candy-filled hands rushing to empty seats sparkling eyes watching trapeze twirling lion roars drowning laughing colorful clowns dancing in sloppy careless circles

#12

deep into hollowed holes
steep stretched escalators test my nerves
i reach the bottom and fear's forgotten
unfolding like sheets of gold leaf
subway walls
and corporate graffiti
replaced by ornate beauty
fountains stages paintings marble
dreamy moonlit towering magnificent
a sparkling atlantis
a treasure chest cavern
hidden and buried in stone

---

phil is missing
                    press of travelers a crowded platform
shouts from behind
                              he's running (frightened)
shouts in russian
                         a red card flashing arms waving

a man steps into his path

blocks
          catches
                    holding

marshie quickly gives directions
                                        and leaves us
chasing phil and his captors

we huddle
a small group in frank's room
trying to joke (for hours)

we hear from phil
he was caught trading money
(five canadian dollars for ten russian rubles)
his captors asked for a signed confession
and a promise to never return

midnight and they return
exhausted

it doesn't feel like spring vacation
it is dark
and close
and cold

#13

tbilisi
far from moscow
where the soviet union is an unwelcome conqueror
rows and rows and rows of georgians surround us
we are packed in with belgian tourists
separated and separate from thousands of soccer fans
we are protected from them
                                        they are protected from us
the belgians beside us are vocal colorful anxious

      georgia vs moscow

here soccer is more than a game

the belgians clap and wave bright scarves
and whistle at each player's entrance
the waves of georgians simply sit and stare and clap
politely
quietly
mindful of the first thirty rows
reserved for the military
a green wall silent and disciplined
                                        unable to move
i try to look in the eyes
of the young ordered soldiers
but they never turn their backs to face us
their faces are lost in trench coats and caps

as we clap and cheer
the belgians' banners slogans and scarves
our western clothes

a tiny dot of color
flickering in a bowl of faded green and gray
i feel georgian eyes glancing staring peeking
envious

the score is tied
a dull rumble of excitement
whispered carefully
passes under and over the stadium

moscow is not loved beyond the thick rows of soldiers

a soccer ball shot
fired and misses
back and forth trampling cleats
a drive toward the goal keep
in the final seconds the belgians are feverish
a soaring arc past outstretched hands
caught in a billowing net

a gun explodes
moscow has lost

we hurry through ignited energy to our bus
surrounded by georgians exuberant in victory
drawing courage from adrenaline
watched by battle-stern green eyes

our bus pulls out
creeping through a thick field of frenzy
our canadian flag taped to a window
spotted by the crowd
who rock our bus and wave and cheer

and for a strange moment
i am trapped inside a glassy cage

#14

an unplanned detour
to escape our tbilisi hotel
its barren rooms and barren bar
drive us into the night
we wander and notice a small opera house

the barber of seville
an amateur cast

our curiosity tugs us inside
three kopeks a person
we tip the coat check with marlboros
(to ensure our coats won't fall on the floor)
we slide into our seats
three rows from the stage
talking in whispers
expecting a circus

the opera begins
charming in chaos
failed octaves missed entrances
stage fright and darkness
politely we watch
feeling pompous and superior
and try not to laugh
the fierce glare of soldiers
ever smoldering behind us

#15

sipping tea in samarkand
a nestled perch
on concrete stilts
an eerie cove
in shadows glow
from sunlight seeping
patterned walls
open air a warmer breeze
so strangely whispers
this hidden space
on kneeling mats and
wooden slats
a simple teacup held in place

#16

we run into green foothills
like the von trapp family
the mountains before us
a wall hiding warring afghanistan
    (fifty miles by crow flight)
dushanbe lit glorious
warmth springing from sunlight
summer bursting outward
fierce from its slumber

we run and gasp through thinning air
tiring quickly
                        breathing sharply
a simple picnic
eaten on boulders
watching the snow line
melt beneath our feet

revived we slide in slush and mud
skiing in sneakers
                              carving trails in liquid grass
we glide toward a small village
hidden in a valley
ignoring our impatient bus driver's calls

the village's houses are frail
                                        precarious
thin sheet metal roofs
                                  barely balanced
                teeter

a naked man stands oblivious
  in a shower without walls
chickens peck at our footprints
  funny and furious

a statue of lenin (hollow plastic)

as small as the village
bolted stronger than rooftops

stands proud and defiant
on a slab of gray concrete

#17

our bus crawls through the streets of tashkent
our intourist guide sits behind the driver
silently pointing directions
the city is frayed and tired
dust gray and crumbling concrete
buildings stacked in even columns blend together
my tired traveled nerves
blurred by a monotone wash of soot

tashkent's lenin square
                                        to our right
another stone-faced assembly line statue
set in concrete
shadowed by local parliament
and ministries

i lose track of our tour
i only hear our guide's words
their bizarre ordered neatness
like the school children of moscow
with staccato closed rhythm
                                                  pure timing and pattern

(i remember her meeting a fellow guide
  for coffee
  drinking and talking in russian
                                                          and english german french and italian
  each word chosen for a particular meaning
  languages drifting back and forth
  for convenience)

in this dull blur of buildings
our guide points one out
proudly
grimy brown from pollution
it seems quite ordinary
but this building
she says
is the ministry of agriculture
painted beautifully brown
the color of earth

#18

another death-dive plane ride
drops us into alma-ata
its skyline smoothed by mosque domes
golden shining brilliant
shimmering beacons playing with sunlight

we drive from the airport
and stop outside a towering dome
its simple golden elegance
draws me toward a darkened doorway
i step silently into cave-like darkness
my eyes searching
                                        patient
as tiled pictures appear dimly
lit from a single doorway revealing
each tiny tile a pure speck of color
tiles blending and blurring
the spinning dome high above me is swirling
a quilt of rainbows and stars
i close my eyes keeping them with me forever

---

we return to the bus
and our tour guide beams
our excited eyes please her
proudly she declaims :
the state has restored
each nonfunctioning mosque
to its original beauty

we ask her politely
could we see a functioning mosque
she takes us
                reluctant
and waits on the bus
impatient
distrustful

two small domes
hidden behind a ten-foot wall in dying sunlight
sad shadows and smeared tiles
grimy gold peel and flakes
a cluttered floor of mud and pebbles
and a single kneeling figure
                                        quiet
                                        simple
                                        functional

#19

for one day we have run out of postcards to visit
we wander without watches
or schedules
through the shops and streets of alma-ata
sidewalk chefs feed us greasy rich deep fried onion treats
a candy cart offers us chocolate licorice cookies
                                                                                                    and vodka
a steamy market free of five-year-plan prices
families bartering fiercely
foreign words fly past me
i clutch my rubles tightly
                                                            feeling the eyes of traders
eyeing me closely

i am overwhelmed by fish and fumes
and step out from the market's canopy
onto a gravel street
i leave our guide's watchful glare behind

dull rippled aluminum roofs
peek over a hill
i walk through blowing dust
past paper-thin houses

our bus tour of mosques
missed this sewery sprawling shanty town
nervous and guilty
i gawk at poverty
feeling eyes at my back

two young girls chasing each other
break through my nerves
their lightly brown faces
smile and laugh
they are tossing a ball back and forth
across gravel
the smaller girl stretches
                                        and reaches
the ball flies over her head
                                            onto my feet
i pick it up
              offer it
shyly she reaches
                        and grabs it

they run away waving
a story to tell

a few feet farther
a voice calls out from the darkness
an arm shoots out from a doorway
fearless (maybe foolish)
i walk over and into
a dark shanty doorway
and stand face-to-face
a young kazakh before me

he's my height and thin and tugs at my jean shirt
i notice behind him (his parents i think)
a man and a woman
a thick stack of rubles
tight in their fists

i look in his eyes
his young dirtied face
i take off my shirt
                                        and stretch it out to him

his head shakes and scribbles
on a scrap of newspaper :

40

i look at it (ready to barter)

50

i write
in large simple digits
he turns and in conference replies

45

happy i circle it
he smiles and nods
rubles in my hand and a shirt on his back

#20

covering the walls of alma-ata

tbilisi samarkand dushanbe tashkent

a little taste of moscow

posters and painted billboards

filled with strength

men and women

eyes lifted upward

hands holding tools and fists

defiant wind-blown banners

words triumphant will and destiny

mandated dreams blaring and blending

#21

pushkin palace outside leningrad
meticulously restored from a wartime siege
room after room after room of gold and spectacle
amazing
postcard
perfect

i'm tired and lean for a moment
lightly
on a palace wall
and am bombarded in russian
by an old man behind me
uniformed and dressed with medals
red with anger
he points at my resting shoulder
our tour guide appears from a corner
their words flurry past me
and the man's voice softens
slightly
the guide turns to me
whispering sharply
i have insulted the dead
the victims of war
by carelessly soiling the walls of this palace

shaken
i apologize softly in english

i stop breathing
for a while
standing silent
touching nothing

#22

we are walking through leningrad
on cobblestone alleys
across bridges and canals
under gas lanterns casting
faraway shadows of royalty and czars
when revolution was merely a whisper

marshie is buying
no wine champagne or vodka tonight
we are going for a special treat

we enter the ice cream shop through an arched stone doorway
where walls of marble surround us
we find seats at a thick oak table
with light sparkling from crystal chandeliers
marshie orders confidently in russian
and he watches our eyes glow
as cool colorful scoops fall magically before us
a shock of flavor
strawberry chills me
i catch a young girl giggling as i shiver
and i am reminded of moscow

i close my eyes for a picture of home
and the foothills of dushanbe appear in its place

i slowly dip my spoon
and feel the cool sweetness pull me into a dream
there are no soldiers
there is no poverty
inside this delicious eden

#23

it's time for our big deal

phil met a fur hat dealer

raoul wants a rabbit cap and caviar

i come along for company
the trader meets us behind our hotel
at midnight
nervously smoking a frail russian cigarette
we give him a pack of marlboros

a cab appears from around the corner
and we crawl inside
cramped together in a rattling car
flying through abandoned streets
our new friend says his apartment is close
but we pass over the same canal three times
(the driver is boosting the fare)
cobblestones are replaced with asphalt and potholes
the marbled ornate spectacle is gone
streetlights are dark or smashed or flickering

we walk in silence to his doorway
our foreign english voices are easy targets
for keen ambitious ears

up a dusty stairwell
inside a grimy doorway

relieved

we drop our coats in his arms
and tiptoe past his sleeping mother
ducking into his close cramped room

he fills our hands with glasses
and a shot of vodka
we smile and clink and wince
in unison
he says he can only stay
in leningrad
if he lives with his mother

he pulls out a box of wedding pictures
women he has married
                                        and later divorced
(for a small fee)
so they too can live in the city

he shows off a shoebox
bulging with postcards and love letters
from faraway tourists

he pulls out three black rabbit hats
we each grab one and run our fingers across smooth fur
raoul and phil barter with dollars
i just sit back and watch
the trader's eyes keen for a deal
his head haloed by an enormous american flag
draped on the wall above him

it is late and we tire
and our trader must go to work (bottling pepsi)
he goes twice a week
                                      for two hours
and the government leaves him alone

our taxi meanders through leningrad streets
and we do not pass a soul
as we wander in darkness

#24

a final aeroflot pilot waits to take us home
we exit through customs
our bags packed
black-market hats flags caviar
unchanged stone-faced soldiers examine us
one by one
staring through our eyes
marshie is taken aside
his suitcase opened and scattered
his interrogator
                    stops
pulls out an address book
and slowly turns each page
searching for names
                    russian names
and writes them down in a small tattered notebook

we watch and wait
as marshie stoops to repack his suitcase
gathers himself his bags
and nervously joins us
a final fiery liftoff and landing
and we hop over the border

helsinki finland

the flight has released us to freedom
i shiver imagining the soldier behind us
searching his country
for the names in marshie's notebook

lost (and found)

i nudge my reading glasses down
watching you rummage through drawers
my glasses, where did I leave my glasses?
you repeat to yourself hoping for an answer

i quietly observe this well-scripted
tightly performed scene on the family room stage
as your fingers fumble until in exasperation
you set down your book and walk away

these things we lose track of
a puzzle piece clinging to a sweaty forearm
an unpaid bill the anniversary card bought last week
a ring of keys all tucked away too safely

i worry most of all about the pages
ripped from a daily calendar on my desk
then crumpled and thrown away
one day closer to a final tear

perhaps next time I should offer you
my reading glasses then lie back eyes closed and
dream of all the things I've lost or forgotten
until in the quiet of night I find what I was looking for

ACKNOWLEDGMENTS

My poetry has benefited from the critique and actionable feedback of many people, starting with my wife and lead editor, Mary, and my father. Ryan, Connie, Marie-Ann, Monique, Marilyn, Linda, Annie, and Patricia helped workshop many of the poems in this collection. Thank you for helping elevate my poetry.

Photo © Kristin Cofer

James Morehead is Poet Laureate of Dublin, California. *canvas: poems* was his debut collection, and he hosts the *Viewless Wings Poetry Podcast.* James' poem "tethered" was transformed into an award-winning, hand-drawn animated short film, "gallery" was set to music for baritone and piano, and his poems have appeared in *Beyond Words Magazine*, *Wingless Dreamer*, *Prometheus Dreaming*, and *PromptPress*. He calls both the USA and Canada home, and is currently based in the San Francisco Bay Area.

Website: viewlesswings.com | Twitter: @dublinranch
Instagram: @viewlesswings | LinkedIn: linkedin.com/in/morehead

CPSIA information can be obtained
at www.ICGtesting.com
Printed in the USA
BVHW082351130322
631391BV00002B/267

9 781736 789025